A D'Oyly Carte Album

A D'OYLY CARTE ALBUM

A Pictorial Record of
the Gilbert and Sullivan Operas

ROGER WOOD

SECOND EDITION

Foreword by BRIDGET D'OYLY CARTE

LONDON
ADAM AND CHARLES BLACK

FIRST PUBLISHED 1953
⌞ SECOND EDITION⌟⌞1958⌟
A. AND C. BLACK LTD
4, 5 AND 6 SOHO SQUARE LONDON W.1

MADE IN GREAT BRITAIN
PRINTED BY R. & R. CLARK, LTD., EDINBURGH

Contents

Foreword

by BRIDGET D'OYLY CARTE

Mr. Wood has had to take to the road to photograph our essentially travelling Opera Company; and I am only surprised that his whole album of pictures is not shown tumbling out of a theatrical travelling basket.

The pictures he has made on his journeyings with us capture something of the friendly human qualities that are inherent in any such living.

Our Gilbert and Sullivan Company might perhaps be called the *commedia dell'arte* of England, representing as it does, a world full of sense, and also of nonsense; a world that appeals to the child at the heart of so many English-speaking peoples the world over.

We have enjoyed knowing Mr. Wood, and it would seem from his sensitive photographs that he has enjoyed knowing us; and I feel sure that this book will give pleasure to all those who follow our adventurings with affection.

Introduction

There are a great many books already published about Gilbert and Sullivan and the comic operas which they wrote together, but there are far fewer books about the people who are carrying on the tradition today and keeping those comic operas alive. Since Richard D'Oyly Carte first invited Gilbert and Sullivan to collaborate in writing *Trial by Jury* in 1875 there has always been a D'Oyly Carte in control of at least one performing company, and during peak periods there have often been several D'Oyly Carte companies touring at the same time.

Richard D'Oyly Carte was succeeded by his wife, Helen, then by his son Rupert who was responsible for the great rebirth of the Savoy Operas after the first world war, and who rebuilt the Savoy Theatre in 1929. Rupert died at the Savoy Hotel in 1948, aged seventy-one, and was succeeded by his daughter, Bridget, who is at present in control of the company.

Among them they have made the name D'Oyly Carte synonymous with fine, authentic productions of the Gilbert and Sullivan comic operas. This picture record of the D'Oyly Carte Company is an attempt to show some of the artists in their most famous roles and also to show by action photographs how the operas look on the stage in actual performance.

My work on this Album, which began in 1952 when I spent some time on tour with the company, has been greatly assisted by the help I have received from both the management and artists of the D'Oyly Carte Company. Miss Bridget D'Oyly Carte has throughout given encouragement and advice, and I would like to thank her particularly for her kindness in writing the Foreword.

In the making of the photographs Mr. Jerome Stephens has been invaluable. By good-naturedly marshalling singers to appear at the right moments for their 'sittings'—hustling the tardy ones and pacifying those kept waiting—by suggesting and checking gestures, costumes and D'Oyly Carte tradition generally, he has greatly contributed to the easy working of what can be a long and trying job.

For the checking of facts and photographs I am greatly indebted to Mr. Stanley H. Parker, to whom I have turned for judgment and information. Mr. Frederic Lloyd has made it possible for me to study the operas in actual performance by accommodating me in theatres that already seemed filled to capacity.

Others to whom I am grateful are Miss Mary Clarke for her very considerable help with the entire text; Miss Ruth Lynam of *Life* magazine, from whose fertile imagination came the original idea for the book; and Mr. Ronald Ingles, M.S.I.A., who helped to choose all the pictures and who made the first lay-out. Mr. D. Graham Davis, Editor of *The Gilbert and Sullivan Journal*, gave me invaluable assistance with the preparation of this second edition.

ROGER WOOD

THE MIKADO

Peter Pratt as Ko-Ko, Lord High Executioner of Titipu:

A personage of noble rank and title—
A dignified and potent officer,
Whose functions are particularly vital!

Four Oriental faces from *The Mikado* : Fisher Morgan as Pooh-Bah, Lord High Everything Else ;
Neville Griffiths as Nanki-Poo, son of the Mikado of Japan and disguised throughout most of the opera
as a Wandering Minstrel ; Ann Drummond-Grant as Katisha, an elderly lady in love with Nanki-Poo ;
Darrell Fancourt as the Mikado himself.

Right: Yum-Yum and her companions Peep-Bo and Pitti-Sing introduce themselves with a song:

> *Three little maids from school are we,*
> *Pert as a schoolgirl well can be,*
> *Filled to the brim with girlish glee,*
>   *Three little maids from school!*

Left to right: Beryl Dixon, Tatiana Preston, Joyce Wright.

Below: Peter Goffin's setting for the second act of *The Mikado*, Ko-Ko's Garden, with Darell Fancourt as the Mikado and Ann Drummond-Grant as Katisha.

Above : The setting for Act I, the Courtyard of
Ko-Ko's Official Residence. Pish-Tush (Jeffrey
Skitch) and the chorus.

Right : Peter Pratt as Ko-Ko : *I've got a little list.*

Pish-Tush (Jeffrey Skitch), Ko-Ko (Peter Pratt) and Pooh-Bah (Fisher Morgan) endeavour to think of someone to behead.

The entrance of Yum-Yum's schoolfellows : *Comes a train of little ladies.*

The Venetian setting for Act I.

THE GONDOLIERS

Below left : Joyce Wright as Tessa and (*right*) Muriel Harding as Gianetta.

Below right : Leonard Osborn as Marco and (*right*) Alan Styler as Giuseppe.

Above: Act I. Don Alhambra, the Grand Inquisitor, with the Plaza-Toros and Luiz

Right: Peter Pratt as the Duke of Plaza-Toro and Shirley Hall as Casilda.

Right: Ann Drummond-Grant as the Duchess of Plaza-Toro and Fisher Morgan as Don Alhambra.

Act II.   A Pavilion in the Palace of Barataria.   *Left to right*: Leonard Osborn, Muriel Harding, Joyce Wright, Jeffrey Skitch.

The crowning of the rightful King of Barataria.   *Centre*: Herbert Newby as Luiz.

IOLANTHE

Above : Ann Drummond-Grant as the
Queen of the Fairies.

Right : The Arcadian landscape of Act I. *Left
to right* : Alan Styler, Ann Drummond-Grant,
Peter Pratt, Ivor Evans, Shirley Hall.

Act I. Phyllis (Shirley Hall) with her rival suitor Earls.

Below left : Fisher Morgan as Private Willis is visited by the Queen of the Fairies (Ann Drummond-Grant) who proves to be not insensible to manly beauty.

Below right : *Faint heart never won fair lady.* Peter Pratt as the Lord Chancellor, with (*left*) Ivor Evans as the Earl of Mountararat and Leonard Osborn as Earl Tolloller.

Joyce Wright as Iolanthe.   Peter Pratt as the Lord Chancellor.

Below : The end of the opera in Palace Yard, Westminster : *Everyone is now a fairy !*

H.M.S. PINAFORE

Peter Pratt as the Rt. Hon. Sir Joseph Porter, K.C.B., First Lord of the Admiralty.

Below : The setting throughout is the Quarter-deck of H.M.S. Pinafore, off Portsmouth, designed and painted by Joseph and Phil Harker. Donald Adams as Captain Corcoran ; Neville Griffiths as Ralph Rackstraw, an Able Seaman ; Darrell Fancourt as Dick Deadeye.

Sir Joseph, who knew nothing whatever about ships, enquires of the Captain (Donald Adams, *left*) whether the crew is well treated. After examining a very small midshipman he comes to the conclusion: *A British sailor is a splendid fellow, Captain Corcoran.*

Darrell Fancourt as Dick Deadeye: *From such a face and form as mine the noblest sentiments sound like the black utterances of a depraved imagination.*

Left to right : Neville Griffiths, Donald Adams, Peter Pratt and Muriel Harding. The ladies' costumes are by George Sheringham.

Josephine, the Captain's daughter (Muriel Harding), is in love with Ralph Rackstraw (Neville Griffiths), an Able Seaman.

THE YEOMEN OF
THE GUARD

Four of the best-loved characters in the Gilbert and Sullivan repertoire. Peter Pratt as Jack Point, a Strolling Jester; Darrell Fancourt as Sergeant Meryll of the Yeomen of the Guard; Fisher Morgan as Wilfred Shadbolt, 'head jailer and assistant tormentor'; Joyce Wright as Phoebe Meryll.

Ivor Evans as Sir Richard Cholmondeley,
Lieutenant of the Tower.

Muriel Harding as Elsie Maynard,
a Strolling Player.

Ann Drummond-Grant as Dame Carruthers,
Housekeeper to the Tower.

Leonard Osborn as Colonel Fairfax.

I have a song to sing, O !
Jack Point and Elsie Maynard (Peter Pratt and Muriel Harding) sing the song of the Merryman and his Maid.

Astounding news !   The prisoner is fled !   Thy life shall forfeit be instead !
Ivor Evans as Sir Richard Cholmondeley (*right*), Fisher Morgan as Shadbolt.   Setting by Peter Goffin.

C

When a wooer goes a-wooing. Phoebe, Jack Point, Elsie, and Fairfax.

The Jester's tragedy. Peter Pratt as Jack Point with Fisher Morgan as Shadbolt.

Left to right : Ivor Evans, Fisher Morgan, Peter Pratt, Joyce Wright, Darrell Fancourt.

PATIENCE

Above: The setting for Act I of the opera. Twenty love-sick maidens, grouped outside Bunthorne Castle and all in love with Reginald Bunthorne 'a Fleshly Poet'.

Right: Peter Pratt as Bunthorne:
> *And every one will say,*
> *As you walk your flowery way,*
> *'If he's content with a vegetable love which*
> *would certainly not suit* me,
> *Why, what a most particularly pure young man*
> *this pure young man must be!'*

Patience is wooed by Archibald Grosvenor 'an Idyllic Poet', in the setting for Act II—A Glade.
The players here are Jeffrey Skitch and Muriel Harding.

Bunthorne, heartbroken by Patience's indifference, puts himself up to be raffled for. As the girls clamour for tickets the Dragoons march around to express their indifference.

Left to right: The Major (John Reed), the Duke (Leonard Osborn) and the Colonel (Ivor Evans), realise there is nothing for it but to dress up and be aesthetic too.

Aestheticism is finally discarded and Grosvenor becomes *a steady and stolid-y, jolly Bank-holiday, Every-day young man. Centre:* Jeffrey Skitch and Peter Pratt.

THE PIRATES OF PENZANCE

Darrell Fancourt as the Pirate King who didn't think much of his profession, but, *contrasted with respectability, it is comparatively honest.*

Opposite, top left: Neville Griffiths as Frederic, the Pirate Apprentice; *top right*: Muriel Harding as Mabel; *below left*: Peter Pratt as Major-General Stanley; *below right*: Ann Drummond-Grant as Ruth, the Pirate Maid-of-all-Work.

Above : Act I. A rocky seashore on the coast of Cornwall. Peter Pratt (*centre*) sings : *I am the very model of a modern Major-General.*

Left : Fisher Morgan, the Sergeant of Police—*Tarantara ! tarantara !*

Below : Act II. A ruined Chapel by Moonlight.
> *Resume your ranks, and legislative duties*
> *And take my daughters, all of whom are beauties.*

Left to right : Darrell Fancourt, Muriel Harding, Peter Pratt, Neville Griffiths, Ann Drummond-Grant, Fisher Morgan.

Act I.   The fishing village of Rederring in Cornwall.   *Centre*:   Fisher Morgan as Sir Despard Murgatroyd and Joyce Wright as Mad Margaret.

RUDDIGORE

Leonard Osborn as Richard Dauntless performs the celebrated Hornpipe which follows the 'Parly-voo' ballad.

Act. II. The Picture Gallery in Ruddigore Castle. Joyce Wright as Mad Margaret and Fisher Morgan as Sir Despard Murgatroyd perform *one of our blameless dances.*

Peter Goffin's costumes for Act II. *Left to right*: Fisher Morgan, Joyce Wright, Ann Drummond-Grant, Ivor Evans, Sydney Allen, John Reed, Shirley Hall.

Above : The Bridesmaids captivate the Gentlemen of the Jury, while the Plaintiff begins to make an impression on the Judge. The Defendant (*extreme left*) suggests a solution : *But this I am willing to say, If it will appease her sorrow, I'll marry this lady today, And I'll marry the other tomorrow!*

Below : The Learned Judge (Fisher Morgan).

TRIAL BY JURY

**PRINCESS
IDA**

Above: Act I, King Hildebrand's Palace. King Gama (Peter Pratt) *centre* with his sons *left*, Guron (John Banks), Arac (Donald Adams) and Scynthius (Trevor Hills). Seated is King Hildebrand (Fisher Morgan).

Below: Melissa (Beryl Dixon) listens unobserved as Psyche (Muriel Harding) sings with Cyril (Leonard Osborn), Hilarion (Thomas Round) and Florian (Jeffrey Skitch).

Above: The end of Act II; Princess Ida defies King Hildebrand. (Victoria Sladen, *centre*, as Princess Ida.)

Below: Hilarion is at last united with Princess Ida. *Left to right*: Florian, Melissa, Lady Blanche (Ann Drummond-Grant), King Gama, Hilarion, Princess Ida and King Hildebrand.

COX AND BOX

Above: Donald Adams (*facing camera*) as Cox and Frederick Sinden as Box.
Below: Cox and Box with Bouncer, their landlord (Ivor Evans).

BACK-STAGE

Japanese hats and China tea. Four of Yum-Yum's school-fellows from *The Mikado* imbibe suitable refreshment between the acts.

Conversation piece, seen through the stairway leading to the quarter - deck of H.M.S. Pinafore.

Behind the scenes, but ever present and ever helpful, is Stage Manager Jerome Stephens. Here he comes forward to assist Lady Jane (Ann Drummond-Grant) as she exits with violoncello in Act II of *Patience*.

A new coat of paint for H.M.S. Pinafore. At the Harker Bros. Scenic Studios in South London, Mr. Joseph Harker supervises the painting of new scenery for the quarter-deck, to replace the travel-worn setting which hangs above.

Rehearsals and performances are only part of the work of Isidore Godfrey, who for so many years has been the permanent conductor of the D'Oyly Carte Opera Company. Here he is seen at the Decca Studios recording one of the operas.

In the girls' dressing-room, Japanese make-ups are applied for *The Mikado* while (*right*) the Officers of the Dragoon Guards relax between the acts of *Patience*.

Gilbert and Sullivan operas are not confined to the professional stage but are performed by amateur clubs and companies all over the world. *Above*: A group of amateurs are seen rehearsing round the piano. Second from the left is Clare Lambert, Secretary of the Gilbert and Sullivan Society.

Below (*left*): The General Manager of the D'Oyly Carte Opera Company, Mr. Frederic Lloyd, talks business with Mr. Stanley H. Parker, the Company's indefatigable Secretary. (*Right*): Miss Eleanor Evans, for many years Director of Productions, has a last-minute conference in the prompt corner with the Musical Director, Mr. Isidore Godfrey.

Constant travelling and frequent performances
are hard on costumes, but the D'Oyly Carte
Company maintains some of the best theatrical
wardrobe workrooms in the country to keep
them fresh. *Right* : Mrs. Blain, the Wardrobe Mistress, inspects the gown of the
Duchess of Plaza-Toro while Miss Ewbank
is busy with an iron.

Below : The highly skilled staff, under the
direction of Miss Ruby Buckingham (*centre*) at
work in the airy and well-equipped workroom.

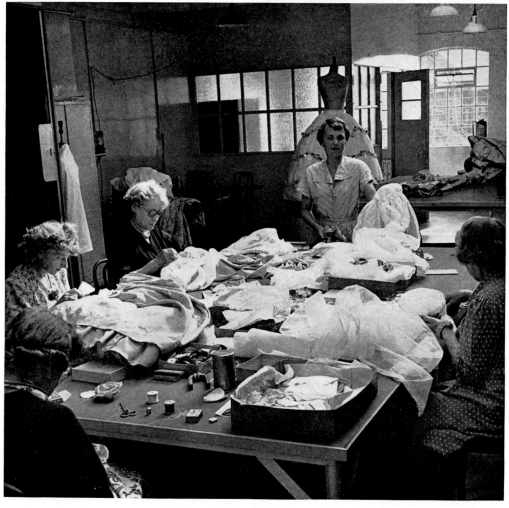

Harry Haste (*right*) is in charge of the D'Oyly Carte workshops and supervises all the giant organisation of transporting the costumes, scenery, properties, fixtures and fittings all over the world. He also sees that everything is kept in good repair and replaced when necessary. With him is another bulwark of the company, Peter Jackson, Storeman.

Below left: Stage Manager Jerome Stephens (*right*) has spent all his life in the theatre and most of it with the D'Oyly Carte Company. He was once in the chorus, knows every detail of the operas and has been affectionately known as Jerry to generations of singers. Here he is talking to his Assistant Stage Manager, Norman Meadmore.

Below right: Bruce Worsley, Business Manager of the D'Oyly Carte Company.

The Mikado

or

The Town of Titipu

First produced at the Savoy Theatre, London, 14th March 1885

CHARACTERS

The Mikado of Japan

Nanki-Poo (his son, disguised as a Wandering Minstrel, in love with Yum-Yum)

Ko-Ko (Lord High Executioner of Titipu)

Pooh-Bah (Lord High Everything Else)

Pish-Tush }
Go-To } Noble Lords

Yum-Yum }
Pitti-Sing } Three Sisters, Wards
Peep-Bo } of Ko-Ko

Katisha (an elderly lady in love with Nanki-Poo)

Chorus of Schoolgirls, Nobles, Guards and Coolies

The plot of *The Mikado* is just an absurd and delightful excuse on which to hang a whole chain of wickedly satirical lyrics. The setting is meticulously Japanese, the spirit entirely English and the mixture is integrated so skilfully that the opera has been, right from its first performance, the most popular of the whole cycle.

The original conception was purely accidental. Gilbert, racking his brains for a new idea, was startled one day in his library by a Japanese sword falling to the floor. It was the spark that was needed ; his imagination went racing off to the topicalities of the Japanese Exhibition at Knightsbridge, to the vogue for Japanese art pots, fans and wallpapers. The original costumes were either genuine ancient Japanese robes or else beautiful Liberty fabrics. Since then the opera has, of course, been redesigned. For many years the settings and costumes by Charles Ricketts, made in 1926, symbolised for Gilbert-and-Sullivan lovers the town of Titipu. In 1953 the opera was given a new production, with new settings by Peter Goffin, which retained the spirit of the opera most successfully.

The plot, Gilbert always maintained, was written with a first intention of providing good parts for the principals of the Savoy company. Be that as it may, it is quite wonderfully contrived and more neatly and gaily worked out than any of the other operas. It all hinges upon a decree passed by the Mikado of Japan in a well-meaning attempt to steady young men and do away with flirting.

This, not surprisingly, leads everyone into trouble. The Mikado's own son,

D

Nanki-Poo, has been forced to disguise himself as a wandering minstrel because Katisha, an elderly lady of the Court, has accused him of flirting, and demanded his hand in marriage. To escape the lady and to escape the alternative, beheading, he has fled from the Court, and has fallen in love with Yum-Yum. Yum-Yum, however, is engaged to Ko-Ko who was once merely 'a cheap tailor', but has now been made Lord High Executioner, the highest rank a citizen can attain. Freshly released from her ladies' seminary, Yum-Yum admits to Nanki-Poo that she does not love Ko-Ko, although, as she is his ward, she doubts if he would let her marry anyone else. Nanki-Poo then confesses his true identity, and they both decide that were it not for Ko-Ko, the laws against flirting and various other obstacles, they could be very happy together.

The Mikado at this point stirs up more trouble by announcing that no executions have taken place in Titipu for a year and unless someone is beheaded within one month the post of Lord High Executioner shall be abolished and the city reduced to the rank of a village. It is looking horribly as if Ko-Ko will have to behead himself, when Nanki-Poo arrives, disconsolate, contemplating suicide with a rope. Ko-Ko strikes a bargain with him. Nanki-Poo shall marry Yum-Yum; at the end of a month he will allow himself to be beheaded and Ko-Ko will then marry his widow. Nanki-Poo and Yum-Yum look forward to at least a month of married bliss, but Ko-Ko remembers another difficulty. The law says that if a married man is beheaded his wife must be buried alive. Yum-Yum decides that she can hardly go through with the ceremony under *those* terms and in the midst of this pretty how-de-do the approach of the Mikado is announced.

Nanki-Poo is threatening suicide again, Ko-Ko is at his wit's end. Eventually he cries in desperation that Nanki-Poo had better marry Yum-Yum and disappear as quickly as possible and he will make an affidavit that Nanki-Poo has been executed, without actually doing anything about it. The Emperor arrives with Katisha, his daughter-in-law elect. Ko-Ko describes the pretended execution with relish, Pooh-Bah confirming it in all his various capacities. The Emperor, unfortunately, has come to look for his son; he is prepared to forgive the mistake that has been made but explains that the conspirators must undergo the penalty for compassing the death of the Heir Apparent, 'something lingering, with boiling oil in it'. To save themselves, Ko-Ko and Pooh-Bah must produce Nanki-Poo, but he will not come forward while Katisha is unmarried. Ko-Ko's only way out is to woo the lady and marry her himself before restoring Nanki-Poo to his father. He goes about it with fervour, melting Katisha's heart with his song about the little tom-tit who died for love singing willow, titwillow, titwillow. Pooh-Bah, as Registrar, hastily performs the wedding ceremony. All is explained to the Mikado and 'nothing could possibly be more satisfactory'.

Nothing could have been more satisfactory to the authors of the opera than the immediate and enormous success it at once enjoyed. It ran for 672 performances at the Savoy Theatre. Since that first production, coinciding with the Japanese Exhibition (there is a reference when Ko-Ko pretends to the Mikado that Nanki-Poo has gone abroad: 'His address?' 'Knightsbridge'!), *The Mikado* has been played all over the world, in many different languages. It was a sensational 'smash hit' in New York from its first performance and started a vogue for oriental furnishings—every smart house had its 'Mikado room'. By the 1940's it was even given in Japan, first by American occupation troops and then by an all-Japanese cast with the Emperor's brother in the audience. It has been filmed in England, it has been given in a swing version by negroes in Chicago, also in a 'hot' version with Bill Robinson as the Mikado, in New York. The popularity remains enormous. With the D'Oyly Carte Company it is still the infallible 'sell out' and stronger than all traditions of how it shall be played are the audience's own traditions of where to demand encores—and where to get them.

Ko-Ko has been played by generations of great players. George Grossmith created him, in a Liberty costume and carrying the very Japanese sword that fell and gave Gilbert the initial idea; Henry Lytton started all that 'business' with the disjointed toe by accidentally tripping over one night and getting a big laugh; Martyn Green developed a tradition of clowning, clowning a little more as the years passed. The present Ko-Ko is Peter Pratt, who makes him a tiny tailor, quite unaccustomed to his exalted station, and looking, as one critic said, like 'a hopeful mole'. For many years the late Darrell Fancourt was the majestical Mikado. He has a worthy successor in Donald Adams.

Nanki-Poo is a gift for handsome tenors; many a girl in theatre audiences has sighed over the wandering minstrel of her generation and when the film was made Kenny Baker had plenty of them sighing in the cinemas too. Neville Griffiths and Thomas Round have carried on this tradition admirably. In wonderful contrast to the comic Ko-Ko, the romantic Nanki-Poo and his royal father, is the ubiquitous Pooh-Bah, symbol of graft and political corruption, clothing all his iniquities in a pompous mantle of ancient lineage and diplomatic phraseology, with a family pride 'something inconceivable'. Sydney Granville played him roundly for years with D'Oyly Carte and also appeared in the film of *The Mikado*. Among the other famous exponents of the part were Rutland Barrington, Fred Billington and Leo Sheffield. Fisher Morgan also carried the responsibilities of all the offices of state (except Lord High Executioner) with magnificent aplomb. The part of Katisha, one of Gilbert's most famous elderly, ugly ladies, is also most rewarding to the actress-singer. Not only does Katisha have a most compelling entrance, she has one of Sullivan's most lovely songs—'Hearts do not break'. The first Katisha was Rosina Brandram. Bertha Lewis played it to Henry Lytton's Ko-Ko, Ella Halman to Martyn Green and now Ann Drummond-Grant towers over Peter Pratt. Yum-Yum is not a particularly big part, for she is usually in company with the two other little maids, Pitti-Sing and Peep-Bo, and the three of them are charmers indeed with their shuffling walk and Japanese hats. 'Three Little Maids from School' was, in fact, the very first of the songs in *The Mikado* which Sullivan composed and at the first performance it was the hit of the show, having to be repeated and establishing from that moment the complete success of the opera.

The Gondoliers

or

The King of Barataria

First produced at the Savoy Theatre, London, 7th December 1889

CHARACTERS

The Duke of Plaza-Toro (a Grandee of Spain)

Luiz (his Attendant)

Don Alhambra del Bolero (the Grand Inquisitor)

Marco Palmieri ⎫
Giuseppe Palmieri |
Antonio |
Francesco ⎬ Venetian Gondoliers
Giorgio |
Annibale ⎭

The Duchess of Plaza-Toro

Casilda (her daughter)

Gianetta ⎫
Tessa |
Fiametta ⎬ Contadine
Vittoria |
Giulia ⎭

Inez (the King's Foster-Mother)

Chorus of Gondoliers, Contadine, Men-at-Arms, Heralds and Pages

The Gondoliers was born in a period of quarrels and bickering within the Gilbert-Sullivan-Carte management. The ill-temper had even infected Gilbert's feelings about the stock company at the Savoy, and he threatened at one time to write an opera with no principal parts so that all the artists would be equal. By the time the opera was produced, however, the storm had blown over and all was friendliness and harmonious collaboration. There is, it is true, a great deal of talk about 'equality' in *The Gondoliers*, but as always in the theatre it needs only a gifted artist to make major and memorable figures of the Duke of Plaza-Toro and the Grand Inquisitor, to say nothing of the two gondoliers and their wives. As for Sullivan's contribution, the music is given freer scope than in the strictly prescribed arrangement of a purely comic opera like *The Mikado*, and he had an opportunity to pour out in melody the impressions which he had absorbed during a holiday in Venice only a few months before he began work on the opera. The eighteenth-century Venetian setting gives scope for a most charming stage picture and elegant costumes and allows Sullivan to use many eighteenth-century measures, for instance the delightful gavotte, 'I am a courtier grave and serious'.

The basic idea, of a state in which all are absolutely equal, is said to have been based by Gilbert on an actual state of affairs in Venice in the fifteenth century. As always, he developed it in a thoroughly topical fashion, making every jibe and taunt entirely applicable to the England of his day and not a few people will think it is more painfully true today than ever before that

> When everyone is somebodee,
> Then no-one's anybody !

The situation arises in *The Gondoliers* on account of the King of Barataria having become a Wesleyan Methodist 'of the most bigoted and persecuting type'. To prevent his son from perpetuating this innovation, the Grand Inquisitor has the child stolen and conveyed to Venice. At the beginning of the opera the Duke of Plaza-Toro, his Duchess and his daughter, arrive in Venice to seek this boy, for the old king has died and the boy must return to his kingdom and to the Duke's daughter, Casilda, who was married by proxy to him in infancy. Casilda is not at all pleased to learn about this marriage for she is in love with Luiz, sole attendant and 'suite' of her impoverished father. The Grand Inquisitor, however, has to admit a slight problem. While there can be no shadow of doubt that the King of Barataria is *one* of the Palmieri brothers, there is complete and irremovable doubt as to *which* of the two it is. The baby king was left with a highly respectable gondolier,

> But owing, I'm much disposed to fear,
>   To his terrible taste for tippling,
> That highly respectable gondolier
> Could never declare with a mind sincere
> Which of the two was his offspring dear,
>   And which the Royal stripling !

To solve the problem it will be necessary to send for Luiz's mother who was nurse to the baby king and will be able to identify him. It is disquieting to the Grand Inquisitor to find that the two gondoliers have just been married. He decides to send them off to Barataria to reign jointly, 'as one individual', until the rightful king can be identified and persuades their wives to remain in Venice in the meantime.

Arrived at Court the brothers put their Republican beliefs into practice, for they believe that, in return for the privileges of royalty they enjoy, the least they can do is to make themselves useful about the Palace. The monarchy is re-modelled on Republican principles : 'All departments rank equally, and everybody is at the head of his department'. This is Gilbert's great opportunity and he develops the whole absurd situation at considerable length, songs and dialogue gaily mingled and all shimmering in Sullivan's warm and lovely music. The 'plot', if such it can be called, is nicely solved and settled right at the end of the opera. Inez, the prince's foster-mother, arrives and explains simply that when the child was stolen from her, she managed to substitute her own child for the royal prince. One of the gondoliers, therefore, is the child of Inez (Gilbert never bothered to explain whether it was Marco or Giuseppe) and Luiz is the King of

Barataria, unfettered by any wife except his adored Casilda to whom he has been married since infancy.

It is the good old Gilbertian solution of babies stolen and/or mixed up in infancy, first used in *H.M.S. Pinafore* and dating back, perhaps, to the occasion when Gilbert himself, at the age of two, was stolen by two Neapolitan brigands and had to be redeemed by an irate father for the sum of £25.

Nobody pays much attention to plot in *The Gondoliers*, however. Audiences are content to sit back and be charmed and lulled by Sullivan's music and to be titillated by Gilbert's wickedly debunking lyrics. As long as there is a comedian in the company to play that 'unaffected, undetected, well-connected Warrior' the Duke of Plaza-Toro, a large and handsome woman for his Duchess, two handsome young men for gondolieri and two pretty girls for their wives, and, in addition, a suave and all-managing Grand Inquisitor, audiences are likely to be very happy with *The Gondoliers*. It was the opera that healed a quarrel between Gilbert and Sullivan with its good humour and beauty, and it continues to distil this warm and friendly spirit.

Iolanthe

or

The Peer and the Peri

First produced at the Savoy Theatre, London, 25th November 1882

CHARACTERS

The Lord Chancellor	Iolanthe, a Fairy, Strephon's Mother
Earl of Mountararat	
Earl Tolloller	Celia⎫
	Leila⎬ Fairies
Private Willis (of the Grenadier Guards)	Fleta⎭
Strephon (an Arcadian Shepherd)	
	Phyllis (an Arcadian Shepherdess and
Queen of the Fairies	Ward in Chancery)

Chorus of Dukes, Marquises, Earls, Viscounts, Barons and Fairies

One of the many amazing things about Gilbert and Sullivan operas is the way one or other of them always seems to have a specially topical appeal, no matter where or when they are being given. Since most of them were written to make fun of (or to cash in on) a topical event of the late nineteenth century, this is the more remarkable and it is a typically Gilbertian topsy-turvy occurrence.

In the Coronation year season at Sadler's Wells Theatre in London, for instance, it was *Iolanthe* which proved to be made to measure for a Coronation entertainment. Most entrances and exits in Gilbert and Sullivan operas are usually made to loud applause, but the delighted ovation for the Peers in the summer of 1953 as they came marching on in full splendour, was not only on account of their own magnificence but because people had been subjected to weeks and weeks of publicity in advance about the different robes of the peers of the realm. Gilbert's insistence in 1882 on correct fabrics and insignia and correct deportment (at one rehearsal he screamed at the peers, 'For heaven's sake wear your coronets as if you were used to them !') paid handsome dividends in 1953, for this pompous, lovesick, lovable troupe were obvious forebears of the magnificent creatures who had been seen by millions, on film or television, participating in the Abbey ceremony.

Topicality aside, however, *Iolanthe* in its present production is proving as immortal as the fairies themselves, even if the fairies at times do tend to look very mortal indeed ! The enchanting romantic nonsense about fairies and peers,

51

with its great big leg-pull of the House of Lords, carried along on one of Sullivan's most charming scores, disarms every kind of audience. The second-act setting of Palace Yard at Westminster, with its dim romantic lighting and large scarlet-coated sentry, in itself always earns a round of applause.

The Lord Chancellor is one of Gilbert's wittiest comic characters. His own legal training allowed him, as in *Trial by Jury*, to extract full measure of fun from the paradoxes of the law, in which he took an especial delight, and when explained in detail by the Lord Chancellor they are found to be gloriously funny in themselves, without it being at all necessary to turn them upside down and deliberately *make* them funny. In addition to all the legal absurdities, for extra measure Gilbert and Sullivan gave him that most brilliant of patter songs (and most difficult of all for the player and conductor to synchronise), 'When you're lying awake with a dismal headache'. The present Lord Chancellor in the D'Oyly Carte Company is Peter Pratt, who contrives to reduce himself to a tiny, shrivelled, almost desiccated creature, weighed down by the robes of office, but with a pair of bright intelligent eyes, a clear, if dry and quavery voice, and, in the most unexpected places, as nimble a pair of feet and legs as have ever skipped and pranced through 'Faint heart never won fair lady'—that show-stopping trio or *pas de trois* in the second act. The other big show-stopper is the song for Private Willis on sentry duty, with which the second act in Palace Yard at Westminster opens. Not only does the audience lavish applause upon it but it is a safe bet that as you leave the theatre you will hear many a middle-aged man still booming away under his breath

> Is either a little Liberal
> Or else a little Conservative !

Gilbert always insisted that it was vitally important for every word to be heard throughout the theatre and this led to some bickering with Sullivan who at times complained that it forced his music into a subservient place, but far more than Sullivan must have complained the singers who have had to cope with Private Willis. To enunciate every word clearly with the chin-strap of your bearskin only just below your lower lip takes quite a lot of doing.

Although she is the cause of all the complications, Iolanthe's is a small part; but it is a rewarding one and it suits Joyce Wright's gentle charm admirably. It is small wonder that the Lord Chancellor is moved by her appeal to him as she kneels at his feet, a suppliant for her son; it is even less wonder that he once loved and married her. For the 'corpulent contralto' of the company Gilbert created the Queen of the Fairies, the character who presides resplendently over the action throughout, getting Strephon the Arcadian shepherd (who was only half a mortal, from the waist downward) elected into Parliament and finally, seeing the end of her fairy kingdom if she enforces the law that every fairy must die who does not marry a mortal, getting out of the difficulty by making everyone a fairy. Embedded in her lovely song 'Oh, foolish fay', is an allusion that might have been expected to date the lyric hopelessly for later generations. Endeavouring to put out the fire of

her dawning love for Private Willis, she calls on Captain Shaw who in 1882 was
Chief of the Metropolitan Fire Brigade :

> Could thy Brigade
> With cold cascade
> Quench my great love, I wonder !

and the chorus repeats his name over and over in the refrain. Today there can
be but a handful of people in the audiences of thousands who have the faintest
notion who Captain Shaw was, but Sullivan's haunting music suffices. As in
other similar cases, it stills even curiosity as to whom the gallant hero might have
been and ensures the immortality of the song. The Queen of the Fairies is one of
the best parts played by Ann Drummond-Grant ; handsome and dominating in
Norman Wilkinson's beautiful costume, she has a voice to match her presence.

H.M.S. Pinafore

or

The Lass that Loved a Sailor

First produced at the Opéra Comique, London, 25th May 1878

CHARACTERS

The Rt. Hon. Sir Joseph Porter, K.C.B. (First Lord of the Admiralty)

Captain Corcoran (commanding H.M.S. Pinafore)

Ralph Rackstraw (Able Seaman)

Dick Deadeye (Able Seaman)

Bill Bobstay (Bos'n's Mate)

Bob Beckett (Carpenter's Mate)

Josephine (the Captain's Daughter)

Hebe (Sir Joseph's First Cousin)

Little Buttercup (a Portsmouth Bumboat Woman)

First Lord's Sisters, his Cousins, his Aunts, Sailors, Marines, etc.

H.M.S. Pinafore was the ship that carried the Gilbert-Sullivan-Carte partnership to its first great international triumphs. *Trial by Jury* and *The Sorcerer* had indeed been successful before but it was the overwhelming success of *Pinafore* that set the three collaborators firmly on the path of comic opera and led to the rest of the immortal galaxy. And yet *Pinafore* nearly foundered right at the beginning of the voyage. It had an encouraging first night but then seemed utterly becalmed during a long spell of hot weather. It was not until Sullivan at a promenade concert conducted a suite from the *Pinafore* score that business began to pick up in the late summer of 1878. Once it did pick up, however, there was no stopping it. All kinds of catch-words and phrases from the opera entered everyday speech ; the popular press worked the gags to death ; 'Pinafore mania' swept the country. The refrain

> What, never ?
> Well, hardly ever !

was the most popular and overworked of all. It still turns up occasionally today, used by people who do not even know the original context.

Considerable spice was lent to the character of Sir Joseph Porter, K.C.B., First Lord of the Admiralty, who had never been to sea, by the coincidence, if one may stretch a word, that at the time of the first performance the First Lord of the Admiralty in Disraeli's Government was Mr. W. H. Smith, founder of the bookselling firm. Disraeli was not amused by the opera, but popular opinion delighted in Sir Joseph Porter, his sisters, his cousins and his aunts, and in no

time the real First Lord was universally known as 'Pinafore Smith'. Leslie
Baily, in his *Gilbert and Sullivan Book*, even recounts a delicious story about
W. H. Smith going to Devonport to launch a ship and being greeted by the band
of the Royal Marines blaring out

> Stick close to your desks and never go to sea,
> And you all may be rulers of the Queen's Navee !

Not only in London was *Pinafore* an overwhelming success. In America the
mania was just as pronounced and pirate and unauthorised versions were springing
up everywhere. It was *Pinafore's* popularity that forced the three partners to
organise their own approved productions of the operas in America (although under
the copyright laws they were powerless to prevent altogether the plagiarising that
went on) and it was also with *Pinafore* that the long and profitable association
with the amateur companies began.

The success of *Pinafore* is not surprising when one considers how gay and
enchanting it still is today, when almost everyone in the audience knows both
lyrics and songs backwards and upside down. When fresh it must have had the
sparkle of champagne, for there is something intoxicatingly gay about both the
lyrics and the music. It pokes fun at the whole British way of life and particularly
at the Senior Service, and deals hilariously with class distinctions which are all
neatly solved by Little Buttercup, the Bumboat Woman, explaining that

> When she was young and charming,
> She practised baby-farming

and mixed two children up, so that Able Seaman Ralph Rackstraw is really of
noble birth while the Captain is of 'low condition'.

In *Pinafore* we find for the first time the prototypes of many of the 'basic'
characters that were to be used again in the later operas. Little Buttercup, for
instance, leads straight to Ruth the Pirate Maid, the Queen of the Fairies and
Katisha, and Sir Joseph Porter, created by George Grossmith, will by the next
opera be transformed into Major-General Stanley, later the Lord Chancellor
in *Iolanthe*. After the success of *H.M.S. Pinafore* the Gilbert-Sullivan-Carte
partnership was firmly drawn up, each of the three to draw an equal share of
the profits 'after all expenses have been paid'. They had their own company
and with this stable basis it was only natural that Gilbert should build his librettos
around the talent available for creating the different characters.

Today *H.M.S. Pinafore* is shipshape as ever and Neville Griffiths does hand-
somely by Ralph Rackstraw, while Peter Pratt is a delightful Sir Joseph Porter,
accompanied always by his sisters, his cousins and his aunts. Ann Drummond-
Grant is a charming Little Buttercup ; while Muriel Harding, looking her best in
the lovely costumes of the period, had one of her best roles as the Captain's
daughter Josephine. Darrell Fancourt will ever be remembered with affection
for his dastardly Dick Deadeye. He has now been succeeded by Donald Adams,
who before was an excellent Captain Corcoran, richly deserving three cheers and
one cheer more for his gallant Captain of the *Pinafore*.

The Yeomen of the Guard

or

The Merryman and his Maid

First produced at the Savoy Theatre, London, 3rd October 1888

CHARACTERS

Sir Richard Cholmondeley (Lieutenant of the Tower)

Colonel Fairfax (under sentence of death)

Sergeant Meryll (of the Yeomen of the Guard)

Leonard Meryll (his Son)

Jack Point (a Strolling Jester)

Wilfred Shadbolt (Head Jailer and Assistant Tormentor)

First Yeoman

Second Yeoman

First Citizen

Second Citizen

Elsie Maynard (a Strolling Player)

Phoebe Meryll (Sergeant Meryll's Daughter)

Dame Carruthers (Housekeeper to the Tower)

Kate (her Niece)

Chorus of Yeomen of the Guard, Gentlemen, Citizens, etc.

The Yeomen of the Guard is the only one of the comic operas that is really a tragedy. Sullivan had been longing for many years to try his hand at something serious and he had been encouraged to do so by the music critics, by many of his fashionable friends and even by Queen Victoria, who had said to him after a command performance of his *Golden Legend*: 'You ought to write a grand opera—you would do it so well.' Gilbert, too, was eager to try something that relied on its genuinely human interest rather than on fantasy and paradox and both men referred to *The Yeomen* in later years as being their best work.

As in the case of *The Mikado*, the inspiration came by chance. Waiting for a train on a railway station, Gilbert noticed a poster advertising the Tower Furnishing Company and it immediately occurred to him that the Tower of London would make an admirable setting for his new opera. He naturally then thought of Beefeaters as colourful figures for his male chorus, comparable to the Peers in *Iolanthe* or the Gentlemen of Japan in *The Mikado*, and at one time intended to call the opera *The Beefeater*. The other alternative working title was *The Tower Warden* and *The Yeomen of the Guard* was not decided upon until shortly before the opening night.

The setting is Tudor, a period which Gilbert loved and which Sullivan enjoyed working on, as it gave him an opportunity to use sixteenth-century arrangements for his songs, the most successful being that haunting madrigal with the 'Tower Green' refrain. Gilbert walked around the Tower for days absorbing atmosphere, and something of its grim history seems to have penetrated the lyrics for they are very different from his usual mixture of farce and mockery.

The mood of the opera is set by the sad little opening song for Phoebe, who sits at her spinning wheel, for 'when maiden loves, she sits and sighs'. Phoebe is in love with Colonel Fairfax who has been imprisoned and sentenced to death for dealings with the devil, the result of malicious reports spread by his kinsman who covets the Fairfax inheritance. Phoebe's father, Sergeant Meryll of the Yeomen of the Guard, is also well disposed to Fairfax and together they plan a means of rescuing him. He shall be disguised as Phoebe's brother Leonard, newly appointed a Yeoman but not yet seen by any of the other members of the Guard, and Leonard shall go into hiding until Fairfax is safe. Unknown to them, however, Fairfax has begged from the Lieutenant of the Tower a last boon before he is beheaded. He wishes to be married, 'to the first one that comes', in order that his estate may not devolve to the malicious kinsman. No sooner is the request granted than two strolling players arrive, Jack Point and Elsie Maynard, and they perform before the assembled crowd the singing farce of the Merryman and his Maid, ironically outlining the tragedy that is eventually to overtake Point himself. The Lieutenant suggests that Elsie should marry Fairfax, who is to be beheaded within an hour, and Point encourages her to do so.

Phoebe manages to secure the keys of the condemned cell from Wilfred Shadbolt, Head Jailer and Assistant Tormentor, who is in love with her, and Fairfax takes his place among the Yeomen as 'Leonard Meryll'. Preparations are made for the execution, but the prisoner has, of course, disappeared. The Lieutenant in fury demands the jailer's life shall be forfeit instead and simultaneously Elsie realises that her husband is still alive ; with nice, unconscious timing, she faints into the arms of the disguised Fairfax. To Point this is a harbinger of disaster and he persuades Shadbolt to say that he shot the prisoner as he swam across the river while trying to escape.

Elsie, meanwhile, has been recovering from shock in Sergeant Meryll's house ; Dame Carruthers, the housekeeper of the Tower, having moved in to take charge of things. During her illness, Elsie lets out the secret of her marriage to the prisoner in the Tower and Fairfax, who was beginning to love her, though unaware she was his wife, is delighted. Point and Shadbolt carry through their bargain and tell a long story about how they have shot the escaping prisoner. Elsie is thus supposedly free from her marriage and both Fairfax and Point woo her afresh ; she chooses Fairfax to the dismay of Point, and also of Phoebe Meryll who, in her distress, admits to Shadbolt that the man who is known to all as her brother is really Colonel Fairfax. In return for his silence, she agrees to marry him. In the nick of time the real Leonard Meryll arrives to announce that Fairfax has been reprieved, and Sergeant Meryll decides that he had better give in and marry Dame Carruthers to stop her asking a lot of awkward questions. Elsie and Fairfax are, therefore, united happily, but two other characters have given only their hands and not their hearts in marriage, and Jack Point, the jester and the most lovable character in the opera, is left with nothing but a broken heart as he sighs for the love of a ladye.

Gilbert was intensely nervous of the effect upon the Savoy audience of this ending and George Grossmith seemed to share the feeling that the audience would never accept a sad ending from him as he had always been known to them in purely comic roles. In the early performances the ending was therefore left indecisive and it was Grossmith's successors, George Thorne and Henry Lytton, who played Jack Point in touring companies, who first brought out the tragedy of the ending. In time, Gilbert realised that this ending was the right one and he is recorded as saying, after seeing Henry Lytton in the part, 'It is just what I want. Jack Point should die and the end of the opera should be a tragedy.'

The setting and costumes for the original production were by Percy Anderson, a well-known artist, but the ones used today were designed by Peter Goffin. The part of Elsie Maynard was created by Geraldine Ulmar, and her singing of 'I have a song to sing, O' with Grossmith as Jack Point, was the great success of the first performance. It is, of course, the melody that immediately springs to mind when *The Yeomen* is mentioned, for it is the theme that runs through the opera, forecasting the tragedy at the beginning and recurring at the end when Point returns to the midst of the merrymaking, a broken man, and begs the company 'attend to me and shed a tear or two'. There are many other lovely songs in the opera, such as 'Temptation, oh, temptation', the justly famous 'When a Wooer goes a'Wooing' and the madrigal 'Strange Adventure'. It is significant that all the most famous songs are either sad or sentimental; they quite overshadow the lusty choruses and the 'character' numbers.

An interesting little footnote to the opera is provided by the fact that in 1891, after Gilbert and Sullivan had quarrelled so bitterly, the stage properties left over from *The Yeomen* were put up for auction. Gilbert bought the axe and the block that had stood on his stage Tower Green and kept them at his house, Grim's Dyke, 'as a relic of the best of our work at the Savoy'.

Patience

or

Bunthorne's Bride

First produced at the Opéra Comique, London, 23rd April 1881

CHARACTERS

Colonel Calverley ⎫
Major Murgatroyd ⎪ Officers of the
Lieutenant the Duke ⎪ Dragoon Guards
  of Dunstable ⎭

Reginald Bunthorne (a Fleshly Poet)

Archibald Grosvenor (an Idyllic Poet)

Mr. Bunthorne's Solicitor

The Lady Angela ⎫
The Lady Saphir ⎪ Rapturous Maidens
The Lady Ella ⎪
The Lady Jane ⎭

Patience (a Dairymaid)

Chorus of Rapturous Maidens and Officers of the Dragoon Guards

The Illustrated Sporting and Dramatic News was at pains to point out after the production of *Patience* that although it might be 'the fashion of the moment' this comic opera could not possibly live. The opera in fact lived through 578 performances in 1881–82 and even today shows no perceptible signs of dying. Wrong as the judgment proved to be, however, it is easy to see how the paper's critic was led into it, for *Patience* is sheer social satire, directed straight at the craze for aestheticism of 1880 and lampooning it in fantastic fashion. The poet Bunthorne was (and still is) made up and costumed as a sort of composite figure of Oscar Wilde, Whistler and Walter Crane. The satire was as topical and as personal as one of Miss Hermione Gingold's *revue* sketches, and by all the laws of the theatre it should have been as dead as mutton within a couple of years.

The expectation of life may, perhaps, have been increased by some kind of interdependence between the opera and the movement it lampooned. When Oscar Wilde went on his lecture tour of America he boosted business for *Patience* ; *Patience* at the same time gave wonderful publicity to Oscar Wilde. The poets who were mocked may now have disappeared in a misty, gas-lit past, but they and their successors have retained an aura of fascination for the young, and there are few people with any knowledge of literature who have escaped a phase of being in love with the 'nineties, with the aestheticism, the decadence, the *fin de siècle* hothouse atmosphere of artificiality in which these people lived and worked. While Wilde and Pater are still read and the period that produced them is studied, *Patience* can be assured of appreciative audiences.

Patience, of course, lampoons the young Oscar Wilde. At the time of its production he was only twenty-five and had published nothing of importance, for *Dorian Gray*, the short stories and the plays were still to come. He was a fantastic young man, not at all unlike Bunthorne, who went around saying he wished to live up to his blue-and-white china, and walked down Bond Street in a plum-coloured velveteen knickerbocker suit carrying exquisite flowers. He was a perfect gift to Gilbert who was able to make him the central figure of a plot that could deride all the ridiculous trappings of aestheticism as it invaded the homes of the would-be up-to-the-minute young women of the day.

The twenty love-sick maidens who sit sighing at Bunthorne's gates when the curtain rises, are dressed in fabrics that themselves echo the designs of the late Pre-Raphaelites, the colours of Burne-Jones and William Morris. A year ago the maidens had all been happily engaged to Dragoon Guards, but now their tastes have been etherealised, their 'perceptions exalted'. Bunthorne, however, takes no heed of the love-sick twenty for he is in love with Patience, a Dairy Maid, the only girl quite unimpressed by his poetry. While the others exclaim, 'How purely fragrant', 'How earnestly precious', she says flatly, 'Well, it seems to me to be nonsense', and one suspects that Gilbert shared her opinion, for the tide turns before the end of the opera and aestheticism is rejected by the whole company. Even Lady Jane, the ageing cellist who loved Bunthorne, deserts him for the Duke, and the Fleshly Poet is, at the end, left with no bride at all and only the sad prospect of having to be content with a tulip or lily instead.

Patience proved almost too big a draw for the Opéra Comique. People were turned away nightly and Carte was not happy until his new theatre, the Savoy, was ready and *Patience* could move there on the 10th October 1881. The Savoy was the most up-to-date theatre in London and, startling innovation, was lighted by the electric light. The production was enlarged and revised for the occasion and the scenery had to be repainted because of the new strong light. Before the opera began Mr. D'Oyly Carte appeared on the stage holding an electric light bulb and explained to the audience the advantages of electricity in the theatre. He received two curtain calls for this little lecture and for the one and only time stole all the honours from Gilbert and Sullivan.

Patience was redesigned for the D'Oyly Carte Company in 1929 by George Sheringham and his designs are still used today except for the costumes of the Everyday Girls which are by Hugo Rumbold. In some ways *Patience* is the most closely integrated of all the operas in that one always thinks of it as a whole, a concentrated attack on what Gilbert thought a very silly social phenomenon. It is probably because of this close integration of plot, lyrics and music that individual numbers are seldom played out of context and there was, in fact, no extract at all from *Patience* in the film *The Story of Gilbert and Sullivan*.

The Pirates of Penzance

or

The Slave of Duty

First produced at the Bijou Theatre, Paignton, 30th December 1879
On 31st December 1879 it was produced at the Fifth Avenue Theatre, New York
The first London production was at the Opéra Comique on 3rd April 1880

CHARACTERS

Major-General Stanley	Sergeant of Police
The Pirate King	Mabel
	Edith
Samuel (his Lieutenant)	Kate General Stanley's Daughters
	Isabel
Frederic (the Pirate Apprentice)	Ruth (Pirate Maid-of-all-Work)

Chorus of Pirates, Police and General Stanley's Daughters

The fantastic success of *H.M.S. Pinafore* in America convinced the Gilbert-Sullivan-Carte partnership that pirate companies (the pun is unavoidable) would be waiting and ready to put on unauthorised versions of their new opera the very minute it opened, so they decided to forestall them by staging simultaneous premières of *The Pirates of Penzance* in America and in England, in New York and Paignton. It was on the New York production that the partners lavished all their attention; the Paignton one was performed by a D'Oyly Carte Company then touring Devon, in a frightful hurry and with very little rehearsal, simply for copyright reasons. The opera enjoyed a great success in New York, but it was not until the following April, 1880, that it was produced in London, at the Opéra Comique.

The Pirates of Penzance followed hard upon *H.M.S. Pinafore* and resembles it somewhat in treatment and in length. The characters certainly bear a strong resemblance to their seafaring predecessors and the aim again was, as Gilbert put it, to treat a thoroughly farcical subject in a thoroughly serious manner. The music, however, is more serious than in *Pinafore* and in several passages it approaches the style of grand opera.

The farcical subject chosen was the plight of an orphan boy, apprenticed to a pirate by mistake because his nurse was hard of hearing and mistook her instruction to apprentice him to a *pilot*. Frederic will be free from the pirate band at the age of twenty-one, but as he happened to be born in leap year, on the 29th February, the pirates point out that he is not really free to leave until he has had twenty-one birthdays. He is stricken with a sense of duty that bids him remain.

A sense of duty is delightfully tweaked by the nose throughout the opera, for Gilbert had no patience with grandiloquent protestations of noble sentiments that

E

ha d no human or sensible substance. He also took pleasure in unmasking other emotions which might hide behind a professed sense of duty. For instance, when Mabel comes forward to save Frederic, the poor wandering one, her friends comment aside :

> The question is, had he not been
>   A thing of beauty,
> Would she be swayed by quite as keen
>   A sense of duty ?

There are three wonderful male parts in *The Pirates*. The Pirate King is a dark dominating figure, and Darrell Fancourt made him ruthless and stern, but jelly in the hands of an orphan. Major-General Stanley (now played by Peter Pratt, following Grossmith, Lytton and Martyn Green), is a 'very model of a modern Major-General' who can 'whistle all the airs from that infernal nonsense "Pinafore" ', but he stoops to a base trick in pretending to be an orphan in order to escape from the clutches of the pirates and thus has an opportunity to sing a melancholy little ballad when tormented at night by his conscience. And finally, of course, there is the Sergeant of Police who makes his entrance with that wonderful chorus, 'Tarantara' and follows it up with a superb song, 'When a felon's not engaged in his employment', with its famous refrain, 'The policeman's lot is not a happy one'. The part is a plum indeed, and, ever since, Fred Billington and Rutland Barrington heavyweights of the D'Oyly Carte Company have revelled in it.

Ruddigore

or

The Witch's Curse

First produced at the Savoy Theatre, London, 22nd January 1887

CHARACTERS

Sir Ruthven Murgatroyd (disguised as Robin Oakapple, a young Farmer)	Sir Roderic Murgatroyd (the Twenty-first Baronet)
Richard Dauntless (his Foster Brother, a man-o'-war's man)	Rose Maybud (a Village Maiden)
Sir Despard Murgatroyd (of Ruddigore, a wicked Baronet)	Mad Margaret
	Dame Hannah (Rose's Aunt)
Old Adam Goodheart (Robin's faithful Servant)	Zorah } Professional Bridesmaids
	Ruth }

Chorus of Bucks and Blades, Ancestors and Professional Bridesmaids

The lot of *Ruddigore* was not a happy one. It followed immediately after *The Mikado*, the greatest success of them all, and it suffered in comparison. Nevertheless, it ran for best part of a year at the Savoy, and Gilbert once said that he alone had made £7000 from the production and sales of the libretto.

The theme is nothing more than a burlesque of old-fashioned melodrama, the sort of thing that had held sway in the theatres in Gilbert's youth, and the niceties of the burlesque are perhaps better appreciated today, now that we are further away from the state of affairs that was common in the English theatre early in the nineteenth century. Gilbert himself thought well of his libretto, although he was not altogether happy about Sullivan's music and at times complained that the ghost music was too solemn. He seems to have become reconciled to this later, however, for under Sullivan's will the autographed score of *Ruddigore* was left to his old partner, Gilbert.

The setting is a Cornish fishing village and it gave Gilbert ample opportunity to indulge his passion for the sea and spatter his dialogue with nautical phrases.

There are many happy touches in the first act: Rose Maybud's silly little ballad with her etiquette book, the pretty duet for Robin and Rose Maybud 'I know a youth who loves a little maid—', the famous Parly-voo ballad for Richard Dauntless and, even more famous, the hornpipe which follows it. Durward Lely, who happened to be a good dancer, was the first Richard Dauntless and stopped the show with his dancing. The hornpipe is now an irremovable piece of the action, and, as performed by Leonard Osborn today, it invariably brings the house down. The chorus of 'professional bridesmaids', fresh and pretty in pink and white, who have an infuriating tendency to burst into

> Hail the Bridegroom—hail the Bride
> When the nuptial knot is tied

at the faintest suspicion of an approaching wedding, is another of Gilbert's inimitable touches of absurdity.

The second act is more serious. The highspot is 'The ghosts' high-noon', and Darrell Fancourt used to sing this magnificently. It was, in fact, one of his favourite numbers in his whole fine repertoire. For contrast, there is the ridiculously solemn duet for Despard and Mad Margaret, 'I once was a very abandoned person', which was beautifully performed by Fisher Morgan and Joyce Wright, and the brilliant patter-trio, 'So it really doesn't matter'.

Ruddigore was out of the repertoire for some thirty-three years after its first production but was revived in 1920 with Henry Lytton as Robin Oakapple. For this revival Geoffrey Toye, then musical director of the company, rewrote the overture and strengthened it considerably. The opera had another misfortune in the second world war when the sets and costumes fell victims to a German bomb. It was restored to the stage in 1948 in charming settings and costumes by Peter Goffin.

Trial by Jury

First produced at the Royalty Theatre, London, 25th March 1875

CHARACTERS

The Learned Judge	Usher
Counsel for the Plaintiff	Associate
The Defendant	The Plaintiff
Foreman of the Jury	First Bridesmaid

Chorus of Jurymen, Bridesmaids and Public

Trial by Jury was the second comic opera on which Gilbert and Sullivan collaborated, but it was the first to be presented by Richard D'Oyly Carte and therefore marks the beginning of the great three-cornered partnership. Richard D'Oyly Carte was at that time managing the Royalty Theatre in Dean Street, Soho, and he badly needed a short comic opera to bolster up Offenbach's *La Périchole*, which was not doing particularly good business. He was a first-rate business man, but at the same time a sensitive man of the theatre and he had long wanted to produce an English comic opera, capable of holding its own with the importations from Paris by Offenbach and Lecocq. Gilbert and Sullivan were both enthusiastic and the whole opera was ready in a few weeks. It is quite short, only forty minutes, and alone of the operas contains no spoken dialogue. There are many people who consider it to be the most perfectly constructed of the whole series and it is indeed a little gem of wit, sentiment and charm. The absurdities that can come out of a breach of promise case, when the sensibilities of the jury and the judge are affected, was just the sort of subject to inspire Gilbert, and the libretto he produced in turn inspired Sullivan to write some of his most sparkling music. The judge in the first production was played by Fred Sullivan, the composer's brother, and he had a great success, for as well as possessing a fine voice he was an excellent comedian. Unhappily he died early in 1876, otherwise he might well have appeared in the whole series of subsequent operas.

Princess Ida

or

Castle Adamant

First produced at the Savoy Theatre, London, 5th January 1884

CHARACTERS

King Hildebrand

Hilarion (his son)

Cyril⎫
Florian⎭ Hilarion's friends

King Gama

Arac⎫
Guron⎬ his sons
Scynthius⎭

Princess Ida (Gama's daughter)

Lady Blanche (Professor of Abstract Science)

Lady Psyche (Professor of Humanities)

Melissa (Lady Blanche's daughter)

Sacharissa⎫
Chloe⎬ Girl Graduates
Ada⎭

Soldiers, Courtiers, 'Girl Graduates', 'Daughters of the Plough', etc.

Princess Ida came back into the D'Oyly Carte repertoire on 27th September 1954, during the London season at the Savoy Theatre. It had been absent for some fifteen years and its resurrection was cause for rejoicing among old Savoyards and the younger generation alike. There was inevitably some criticism of cuts in the text, of over-dressing, of casting policies, all that the Gilbert and Sullivan enthusiast means by 'breaks with tradition'. On the other hand, everyone was pleased to have *Princess Ida* back, and the general wish was that it should be played frequently until it was once again firmly established in the affections of the public and as familiar as the more steady favourites. As W. A. Darlington remarked in the *Daily Telegraph*, on the first night of the revival, 'the theatre seemed to be full of people telling each other that this is Sullivan's best score'.

Princess Ida had a difficult birth, a rather unhappy childhood and has suffered long periods of neglect during her life. It is greatly to be hoped that she is now entering a happier phase and will enjoy the popularity she deserves.

Gilbert called the opera 'a respectful perversion' of Tennyson's poem *The Princess*, and the description is apt. *The Princess*, to most people today, suggests 'The splendour falls on castle walls' or 'Tears, idle tears, I know not what they mean', for the songs inserted in the narrative have become so well known that they have eclipsed the poem itself. But the characters and plot of *Princess Ida* come almost intact from Tennyson's story within a story, and Gilbert followed him also in writing the dialogue in blank verse. The opera was written at the time when women's colleges were of very recent foundation (Girton opened its doors in 1872 and Newnham followed in 1875) and the idea of university education for women was still a fairly fresh joke One would expect the joke to have faded by today, but the basic idea—of a household of one sex attempting, in the interests of scholarship, to deny the other entry—is never likely to lack theatrical possibilities. (In reverse, it served Shakespeare himself very nicely in *Love's Labour's Lost*.)

Sullivan wrote the music at a time when he was battling against ill health and out of sympathy with comic opera. He had been forced to abandon an invitation to write a second symphony for the Leeds Music Festival because of of the work entailed on *Princess Ida* and he felt he was neglecting his true gifts. The conflict of interests was doubtless aggravated by his health, the looming spectre of a deadline by which *Princess Ida* had to be completed, and by growing irritation with Gilbert, but these considerations in no way affected the quality of his music.

Princess Ida comes as near to Grand Opera as any of the Savoy galaxy, and Ida's invocation to Minerva

> Oh, goddess wise
> That lovest light,
> Endow with sight
> Their unillumined eyes

was always spoken of as being in the nature of Grand Opera until in 1954 it was sung by an operatic soprano, when everyone decided that something far simpler and fresher was required. Sullivan may have drawn inspiration from Tennyson for his more serious passages, but the comic parts are as brilliant as ever. As far as the music is concerned, both audience and critics, like King Gama, have nothing whatever to grumble at.

The strain had been so great, however, that Sullivan fainted after the first performance and was seriously ill for several weeks thereafter. As soon as he recovered he wrote to D'Oyly Carte to say he would write no more comic operas, and even when it became necessary to find a successor to *Princess Ida* he remained adamant, turning down all Gilbert's suggestions for a new libretto. The correspondence between the two men grew increasingly bitter and it seemed as if the end of the partnership had been reached. Then Gilbert had the idea of *The Mikado*—and Sullivan accepted it by return of post.

King Gama was created by George Grossmith and was later a favourite part of Henry Lytton (who made his first appearance in Gilbert and Sullivan at the age of seventeen in the chorus of *Princess Ida* under the name of H. A. Henri). Peter Pratt, in 1954, was a worthy successor to these illustrious predecessors. Fisher Morgan was comfortably at home as King Hildebrand ; Thomas Round, then a welcome guest from Sadler's Wells and now happily back in the D'Oyly Carte Company, was an excellent Hilarion; and Ann Drummond-Grant, a former Princess Ida, was inevitably—but happily—cast as Lady Blanche. Victoria Sladen sang Princess Ida in London. She sang beautifully (particularly 'I built upon a rock'), but the general verdict was that she was miscast and had not had time to acquire the very individual style required by Gilbert and Sullivan. Later the part was taken over by Muriel Harding who seemed more at ease and was more successful. Now it is sung by Jean Hindmarsh.

Cox and Box

First public performance, 11th May 1867

CHARACTERS

Cox (a Journeyman Hatter)   Box (a Journeyman Printer)   Bouncer (their Landlord)

Cox and Box is the only opera in the D'Oyly Carte repertoire which is not by Gilbert and Sullivan. It was Sullivan's first work for the stage and was originally written for private performance at an evening party given by the dramatist F. C. Burnand. Burnand wanted to use Maddison Morton's farce *Box and Cox* for a comic opera and hit on the happy idea of inviting Sullivan to compose the music. Sullivan was interested equally by the opportunity to try his hand at something new and also the chance to have the result given at one of Burnand's fashionable parties. The opera was first performed at 11.30 P.M. on the evening of 27th April 1867, with George du Maurier as Box, Harold Power as Cox and Johnnie Forster as Bouncer. It was later revived for a charity performance and seen by German Reed who acquired it for his Royal Gallery of Illustration in Lower Regent Street, as a work suitable for respectable audiences. It ran there for 300 performances and its success undoubtedly encouraged Sullivan to continue writing for the stage.

During the great period of D'Oyly Carte revivals of the Savoy operas after the first world war, *Cox and Box* was restored to the stage with another distinguished cast, namely Darrell Fancourt as Bouncer, Sydney Granville as Cox and Leo Darnton as Box. It continues in the repertoire today, the traditional curtain-raiser to *H.M.S. Pinafore*, and still delights with its merry martial tunes and nonsensical story.

The D'Oyly Carte Organisation Today

The operas illustrated and described in this album are the works of Gilbert and Sullivan which comprise the current repertoire of the D'Oyly Carte Company and which have proved the most popular throughout the years. They have been seen by literally millions of people not only in England but throughout the world, for ever since the first expedition to America in 1879 when Richard D'Oyly Carte, Gilbert and Sullivan took their 'authentic' production of *H.M.S. Pinafore* to New York, performances have been welcomed just as enthusiastically in overseas countries as in England. The peculiarly English mixture of wit and sentiment, oil and vinegar, has seemed equally delectable in all countries from America to Australia, from Germany to Japan.

The D'Oyly Carte Company has kept companies touring in England and overseas almost continuously since the 1870's, and by making the operas available for performance by amateur societies they have helped to make them familiar to millions more people in operatic societies throughout the world. As Lord Onslow said in 1907, 'Throughout the whole of Sir William Gilbert's writings there is not one single word that might not be enjoyed by the most innocent member of society', and this simple fact has made them eminently suitable fare for the young. Whole generations of theatre-goers look back on their earliest visits to the theatre to see *The Mikado* or *The Gondoliers*, and they are still first favourites for end-of-term performances in schools—not only in England but in America too.

The Gilbert and Sullivan Society was founded in 1924. It keeps all these lovers of the Savoy operas in touch with the D'Oyly Carte Company and also with the activities of amateur groups. It arranges meetings and lectures and it issues a *Journal* which is a mine of history and information about matters Gilbert and Sullivan. The address of the Society is 273 Northfield Avenue, Ealing, W.5, and the Honorary Secretary, Miss Clare Lambert, is always delighted to hear from new enthusiasts.

From the very beginning there seems to have been something rather special about the Gilbert and Sullivan audience. Affection for the comic operas drew people closer together into some sort of brotherhood or society. As early as 1890 the *Illustrated Sporting and Dramatic News* was calling the Savoy audience 'a congregation' and the peculiar devotion shown by this special audience has always puzzled outsiders. Its loyal support has been a very precious factor in keeping Gilbert and Sullivan alive, but at times it has come near to killing the operas with kindness, as when encores are demanded again and again (for no very special reason except that a certain verse always *has* been repeated four or five times), and when change and a fresh approach in production are opposed simply because they are a change. The worst that your rabid Gilbert and Sullivan fan can say of a performance is 'It's *different*'—but these two words are uttered in tones of contempt, disapproval, sorrow and anger calculated to shatter the resistance of the most intrepid manager or producer!

Nevertheless, the D'Oyly Carte management has always recognised that to keep the productions absolutely unchanged would be to turn them into defunct museum pieces. Fashions change, figures change, costumes must be cut differently. Settings need replenishing, stage deportment changes with the years. It was Rupert D'Oyly Carte who made a clean sweep of dead tradition and shabby, dated costumes when he took control of the company after the first world war and built it up for that great London season at the Princes Theatre in 1919. The present management is just as sensible of this need to maintain standards of production, and the company possesses some of the best theatrical workshops and wardrobes in England. They are situated in South London and there a large staff of devoted and highly skilled people, many of whom have virtually grown up with the D'Oyly Carte Company, see that settings are freshly painted and in good repair, that costumes are spick and span no matter how many miles they have travelled.

The basic ten operas have been kept in excellent repair and in 1954 *Princess Ida* was rescued from temporary exile and given a handsome new production.

It would be an exciting and rewarding experience to see some of the other operas, staged authentically by the D'Oyly Carte Company. For instance, *The Sorcerer* (first produced 17th November 1877), which introduced George Grossmith in the character of John Wellington Wells, 'a dealer in magic and spells', and ran for 175 performances. *Utopia Limited* was a late opera, following *The Gondoliers* in 1893, and it ran for 245 performances. It exploded every possible solemn sentiment of Victorian life and was set in a South Sea island, turned into Utopia by a reformation based on the British way of life, with six representatives of British culture as models. Revivals have been contemplated, but the complexity and costliness of the production have dissuaded former managements. It would be a great service to the musical stage if the D'Oyly Carte Company could put on an 'authentic' revival before the copyright lapses, in order to set a standard for the future.